On Being Seventeen

Aarya Chavan

Copyright © 2022 From Aarya

All rights reserved. No part of this book may be reproduced or used in any manner without written permission of the copyright owner except for the use of quotations in a book review. For more information, address: from.aarya@gmail.com

First Edition

Cover by Prutha Chavan

ISBN 978-0-578-37950-0
Library of Congress Control Number: 2022922658

Contents

On Youth	1
On Chaos	23
On Beginning	45
On Love	69
On Legacy	91

On Youth

When you're seventeen,
You can't expect how often you will
fall
become heartbroken
lose sight of where you are
But even if you knew
Wouldn't you still walk the same path?

My heart breaks
for the memories that could have been made

My heart aches
for the words that could have been spoken

My heart makes
too much space for those who have already left

I didn't survive my childhood
I'm still haunted by it
I'm still trying to get past it
I'm still trying to live in it

I haven't moved on
I'm not celebrating my triumphs
I'm still mourning my losses

I still feel like a child
A child that's been pushed into the world
Who now has to fend for herself
Figure everything out by herself

I'm not ready to face the world
But
Who ever is?

Oh, how beautiful is the heart
If only I could see it in the mirror

I'm tired of apologies and victims
I feel sick to my stomach when I think of them
I want vengeance and no mercy
I won't go halfway anymore
I'll drink my poison
After you drink yours

I'm afraid of losing a life
I have only been longing for
What if I will be disappointed?
What if I will never be satisfied?
Maybe that's why I never chase after it.

The only thing she wanted
was to be by your side
And yet it was by your side
that she felt the most alone

You used to be my friend
You used to call my name
You used to think of me
And I used to know when I occupied your mind
But now when I think of you
I wonder if you think of me still

I have run after you
for as long as I have known

But now my legs are tired
They have lost strength

So will you,
will you come to me?

"Why do you fall so easily?"

Because that way I'll only be pushed once.

Tragedy begets woe
Woe begets inspiration
Inspiration begets creativity
But all that is useless without motivation

Unfortunately I don't have much motivation
I feel so lost without creativity
Because I need creativity to feel alive
And I need to feel alive to avoid another tragedy

Oh, cruel irony

I hurt people because I'm so desperate for them to know how much I hurt
I love people because I'm so desperate for them to love me back

There are so many things that remain unsaid
I thought I would see you again
And I wanted to tell you
I didn't know it then but I do now
I want to go back in time just to tell you
But I'm afraid I'll forget when I see your face
Maybe some things are better left unsaid
After all
What would change?
Would you love me more if you knew?
And if you loved me more would I feel whole?
The words on the tip of my tongue escape me
But I'll learn not to regret
My mind forgets but my heart leaves space for those forgotten words
And if I see you again I'll...

The fireflies that stop by my window at night
That give me light for just a moment
They give me hope

"Are you proud of me?
Have I made you proud?"

I ask with eagerness and desperation
But no words come

But then I realize that the answer is simple

"Yes, I am proud."

The words come out of my own mouth
They're the only ones that matter anyway

She smiles
Her face glows with the radiance of
a thousand suns
But she doesn't yet know of sadness, grief, regret,
and of gloom that never stops

And no matter how much you try to warn her
try to prepare her
try to change her
She'll never stop smiling
Because she already knows it won't last forever

So she smiles

The words from an old book greet me like a friend
I feel a familiar smile creep onto my face
as I remember the journey I had gone on
Like friends we partake on another
Like friends we part once more
The wonders of an old book
never cease to remind me
of simple pleasures and beautiful memories

Nostalgia comes to comfort me
If it was a good memory,
I feel comfort in having been somewhere
and having been okay
If it was a bad memory,
I feel comfort in passing that moment by

Nostalgia comes back to me
in music, scents, places, and people
It's like watching a younger me live again
Not having known or seen
The things I have now
But still being able to exist beside me

Nostalgia comes to remind me
Of where I was
And of how I got here
Of what I gained
And of what I lost

Nostalgia tells me my name
And tells me to never forget
Who I am

And though it may be hard
You go through it anyway
Because it's worth it

Knees covered in dirt and blood
Heart filled with hope and love
I look on ready to face the world

On Chaos

My pen comes back empty
after I dip it into the ink.
I wake up after a long night
of pouring my heart out,
and the pages are still blank.
Can anyone tell me what I've been trying to create?
Can anyone find what I've lost inside me?

Freedom does not come beautifully
Freedom comes from dirt and death
Freedom makes people cry and scream
But freedom must be worth it
if through all this we yearn for it
If I'm left bleeding and dying
If my screams sound like songs
I'll keep fighting for freedom

There are times when I feel
that the world won't stop for me
When I feel that I'm being dragged to a finish line

There are times when I feel
that I am drowning
When the air is only inches away from my head
When I'm thrashing around because I can't swim
When I feel that if I stop for even a second
I won't ever breathe again

But I'm not being dragged
And I'm not drowning
And yet I can't breathe
So what should I do?

You lack emotion just like me
We're not monsters because we crave something different
You say you know me but we're strangers now
The only kinship that exists is between shadows
You can forget me
it's okay

Let me explode
Let me tell the world of the pain I'm in
Let me scream it and cry it
And when the tears come
know that it won't stop
That it's not enough
That it'll never be enough
The torment my heart knows of
cannot be embodied or forgiven
or forgotten

Let me release

And then lay me down
And let me rest
Because after all this
After I lament and regret
And tell the world that it should be sorry

Let me be

How I long for simpler times.

So many writers refer to their suffering

as though they were drowning

I don't suppose many writers

have experienced drowning

but perhaps we all suffer in the same way

I've been holding my emotions inside for so long
I forgot what they look like.
Maybe they'll come pouring out of me
like a hurricane.
Maybe I'm stronger than I think.

I feel as if to speak
is to carry your words into existence
I feel that if I were to speak of my suffering
I would bring it into this world
I feel that if I keep silent
my darkness would never rise from within me
and wreak havoc
on my fragile foundation

And so I write
To keep my sorrows contained
To let them exist without existing in me
I write
so I will be at peace

There are some days when
I want to break all that I see
But when I look in the mirror
I see a person who's already in pieces

"You can't have everything." They say.

But,
I don't want everything.
I don't want to own
all the possessions in the world.
Nor do I want everyone
to look at me all at once.

I just want a peaceful quiet in my mind
and a space to be
where I can see no sadness.

I look around and see no one but myself.
Where are all the people I love?

The depths of my mind scare me
I blur my focus
I ignore and avoid and fight myself
and I'm afraid
Afraid that if I look inside my mind
I'll see someone else
Someone unfamiliar
Someone telling me that
this is who I really am
or who I was supposed to be
And I'm afraid I'll become lost
That I won't know where to find myself
But who am I if I don't know
what's inside my mind
I am already lost

You've already left me
Don't come back with lingering feelings
Let me be at peace
Leave me
Or I'll leave you

There are moments when life hits me all at once
when my lungs are emptied
and my heart is shaken
And I have to stop everything I'm doing
to lift my mind from the ground
to put the pieces back together

When I'm done and rested
I hope to resume what I was doing
But I look around
and I'm unfamiliar with what I see

A hurricane had hit and my reality had fallen
Life did not wait for me

Now I must regain my footing
in this unknown landscape
It's daunting to try to catch up
I worry that I will fall again and watch my life
run farther from me still

But when the hurricane comes again
the winds push me forward
even if I don't want to move

The only feeling I've been able to muster up
in these painfully long and dreary days
is a heartache

I tell myself to wait
To wait until I'm alone
Until it's safe to be
To be myself
To come out of my shell

And so I wait
I wait as moments and people come and go
I wait for the day to end
And then for the darkness to leave me too

But as I wait
I look out and I see
the people I could have become
and the things I could have learned
I see it all pass by

I hope that when I'm done waiting
When I come out of my shell
When I finally feel safe
I'll be able to be
Just be

My heart hurts in a way that tells me
I loved,
        I lost,
                and I lived

No matter how hard I try to fill this void
Somehow it's never enough

Well I'm done feeding my hopes and memories
to an insatiable darkness

On Beginning

You want to keep going
You want to get out
But your grief is heavy
and your hands are bleeding
Stop for a second
Let go
Release
And then begin again

You will hurt
like you never have before
You will grow
in places you never thought you would
You will regret
the things you said you never would
But you will keep going
And you will be okay

What do you want from the world?
What is it you think the world owes you?
An apology?
Redemption?
A second chance?
What is it you want from the world
That you feel the need to reopen
your wounds
your hurt
your scars
When will you accept
that you're not being hurt anymore
that you're safe
And that you can leave your misery behind you
Make room for the love you deserve

I remember you
You who is so familiar
You who was so angry with the world
who longed for justice
who longed for peace
I remember how you stayed bright eyed
despite all the misfortune
despite all the pain
I feel lost without you
I miss you

But
then again
I'm glad you moved on
I'm glad you're healing
I'm glad that I can be here now
Because without you I wouldn't

(Cont.)

When I look in the mirror,
I don't see you anymore
I don't know where you went
but I remember you
I remember your eyes
your frown
your strength
You stayed so strong
You stayed strong for me
Know that you are in my heart
and that you'll always be in my heart
Because I remember you
and I'll never forget you

I looked into the unknown
knowing I'll be alright

I thought I wanted others to know me
But maybe I just wanted to know myself

I don't remember what being at home feels like.
Yet I trust that I'll know when I'm home

How is it that after you tried to silence me
I became louder
that after you tried to change me
I remained steadfast
that after you tried to hide me
I became brighter
If that isn't strength I don't know what is

If you start to hide yourself from others
it will not be long before you become hidden from
your own eyes

There are so many memories to be made
But my mind only dwells on those of the past

Don't come near me
Don't let me be idle
Don't sway my heart
Don't let me crumble
Don't get hurt
Don't let me see you
Don't look for me
Don't let me love you

Forget everything that happened
Forget the pain
Forget the regrets
Move forward with hope in your heart
And perseverance in your soul
Move forward only holding yourself
Yourself is all you need anyway

And all of a sudden
My world had changed
I was standing in unknown territory
And I couldn't go back
I didn't know what to do
But when I looked to the horizon
I think I saw you
So I kept walking forward

I find myself at the start all over again
Even after I've come so far
I must begin again

The path I must walk on looks the same
The edges and imprints are so jarringly familiar
And yet I cannot predict how this journey will be
If I'll come out of it a new person
If I'll have to begin again

Again

No matter how much I prepare
No matter how much I predict
I will have to face this day
And all days after this
With the same courage and resilience
I needed yesterday

I've seen your scars

And I've seen your wounds

Your heart refuses to show itself

But I know how loudly it beats still

Frozen in place

You think you're protected

Head down, out of sight

You wish to be forgotten

But you're here nonetheless

You still wish to bear the weight of the world

Your eyes still open to see how far is left

Feel the tenacity in your blood

It's there, I swear

Carry on, child

This is your world

Sometimes I close my eyes
and just wish that when I open them again
I'll be somewhere else.
Anywhere else.
But something deep inside my heart
tells me that
I'll miss the comfortable hell
that is my present residence.
And I just wonder when it'll be
that I'll be able to leave
with no regrets
and no lingering feelings.
I want to be brave enough
to walk out of my house without an umbrella
and welcome the rain with open arms.

The happy moments never seem to last

But

then again

neither do the unhappy ones

Look up

Look outside

See how the world moves on

And you can too

Your shelter may soon enough become your prison

So stand up

Remember your pain but do not get lost in it

Brave the darkness and embark on your adventure once more

The world you've created inside your head
is vast and incredible
But open your eyes dear girl
and make your fantasies a reality

On Love

Love isn't the medicine that heals your ailments
it's the hand that feeds you the medicine
and dresses your wounds

I've written many things
all of them for you
But I've moved on
from writing about you

And now
I'm at a loss for words
My page is blank
My pen is slipping

But I don't want to stop trying
Because then I'll have nothing to do
but think of you

What is courage if not the ability to love again
despite the pain that's been caused?
If that is foolishness then call me a fool.

Holding on to your passion is like
Holding on to a rope in a waterfall

Unbearable yet thrilling

Holding on to someone
when you don't know if they'll return is

Unbearable yet thrilling

I break, tear, and rip
at the soft skin on my chest
so that maybe
you can see how big my heart is

You love

        and you love

                and you love again

But it breaks my heart
when no one loves you back

Let me hold you

Let me tell you that you matter

Let me give you a shoulder to cry on

Let me show you what real love should look like

You are my muse
And until I find a new one
I will continue to create you
over and over again.

Being with you makes me want to think out loud.
That's quite a compliment if you didn't know.

Do you know?
Do you know that I'm thinking about you?
That I'm thinking about that moment?
That it's all I think about?

You're all my mind encompasses.
I hope you know.

The memory of you has faded
But the feeling of you in my arms
has not escaped me for a second

Even if we never meet again
I'll always love you
because of the way you loved me
when I didn't feel enough

The people who love us don't leave us

If you want to be sentimental
I'll tell you that they're
in our thoughts and our hearts

If you want to be superficial
I'll tell you that they're
liking all our social media posts

If you want to be hopeful
I'll tell you that they're
somewhere on the path we're walking on
They're either walking beside us
or waiting up ahead

And so we'll see them again
One way or another

It's so lovely

how you cross my mind

It's so lovely

how you smile

I want to be

all that you are to me

Even if all you can do
is rip up the words I've said to you
to create your own sentences
I'll still love you.

Matters of the heart
can turn even a wise man into a fool.
Who am I to tempt that fate even if I'm not wise?
The lure of an illuminated and unpenetrated mind
cannot compare.
And so, I would trade anything to obtain
a foolish type of love.

Your eyes are like the ocean

Not in the way that they are a

captivating blue-green color

But in the way that I want to drown in them

I'm having dreams of you again
Is it because you're thinking of me?
Is it because I can't stop thinking of you?
Is it because I've been so busy all day
that you come to me at night?
I can't see you so I can't ask you
But as long as I dream of you every night
I'll be okay

It's the birds that remind me of day
And the silence that reminds me of night
But you remind me of home
And what it means to feel right

It only takes one moment

That moment

When you reach out

And decide to change everything

On Legacy

Sometimes I feel
like my past disappears behind me as I age
like I have nothing to go back to
and nothing to remind me of who I was

And so I'll leave a trail
a trail for myself to look back on
and for others to find
to lead me back to if I get lost

I am spending a lot of time thinking about
the words I write and the life I live.
And I've come to realize
that they're about the same thing

It's surprising
The things I do that contrast with what I think
It's like my mind and body
are two different people
It's like I don't know myself at all
It's confusing
And yet reassuring
that I can change at a moment's notice
that I'm not limited
to who I was

I can feel the passion bursting through my skin
If only I was strong enough
to let it out strategically
Maybe then I could control my creation
rather than be controlled by it

I just want to create something beautiful

If only I could retire into
the soft sunlight and mellow grass
If the slow crashes of ocean waves
onto an empty beach could be heard
I would sit for hours and wish to never leave

The pain of living is nothing compared to

the pain of losing

If I become silent

what will you miss more

My words that never ceased to fill the air?

Or the sound of how I said your name?

So kill me
Come here and kill me
And once you're done,
clean your mess
Try and wash my blood off your hands
Hide your weapons and hide your crime
But know that the world will forget your name
and mine will live on
The legacy that you tried to erase will live on
The last thing you'll see is my smile
and it'll live forever in your head

I'd rather have a friend to count on
than a God to believe in

I am not unlovable
No
Please don't judge me by the amount of people
who choose not to be with me
I am unattainable
I am unfathomable
I am lovely and I will love you too
So do not call me unlovable
Do not believe the silence of others
Over the screams of my soul

I crave people
I crave the knowledge that I'm not alone
I long for someone to talk to
For someone to sit with me and listen
to the stories of what my heart has weathered
I want so much to be loved
that I hold on to someone who doesn't love me
I thought that when they saw me
When they looked into my eyes
They would love me enough to want to put
the pieces of my broken heart back together
It was foolish of me to want someone
in order to feel complete
But what's the point in living
if I have to live alone?
I'm not here to amass objects and trophies
While gold looks pretty
it hangs cold upon my chest
I want to hold someone's hand
and laugh among friends
I want to get lost in a crowd
and I want someone to come and find me
to want me
I'm here to love and be loved

As I sit with myself
I feel my body grow sadder and sadder
But the music
The music makes me feel
like nothing else matters
Like it'll all pass
And it'll all be okay
As long as I have music

If there is one thing you should know about me
It's that I never stop trying
Even when I'm still
My mind is occupied by a thousand thoughts
on how to be better than I was yesterday

In my room
I have broken bottles and lost objects
I have incomplete sets of a bit of everything
I have tattered dreams written down in
tattered notebooks
I hold the motley collection
in the hopes that they can make me whole

On my nightstand there is a candle
It had been burning since I have begun writing
If it could talk, what would it say?
Would it tell of the painstaking journey
it has watched me go on
Would it recall the color of my blood
as I poured my heart onto the pages
Or would it speak of the words
I removed from my manuscript
the ones I tried to hide from the world
I wonder

I was born in August
August feels like Sunday
in that you're savoring it for as long as you can
until the inevitable Monday comes
But I wasn't born on a Sunday
No, I was born on a Monday
It was inevitable that I would come

Sometimes I wish people would like me
as much as they like Fridays
But I'd rather be powerful enough
to occupy everyone's mind
like Mondays do when it's the weekend
I'll leave if you'd like
as Mondays do and Tuesdays come
But I'll come back
and you'll know when I do
I am inevitable

My heart is a book filled with lengthy words
and crude drawings
Dare to read it and dare to love me
Attempt to burn it and its ashes will
attempt to burn you

My heart is a cavern waiting to be occupied
Whether a single torch or many is lit
I will be warmed nonetheless

My heart is a stone cast into the ocean
Worn down by the unforgiving waves
Forgotten in the dark blue depths below

My heart is the moon shining above you
Alone but never lonely
The object of many's desire

When you see
my footprints
my fingerprints
my lipstick on the edge of my cup
the bent corners of the pages
in my favorite books
the faded color on my pillowcase
the empty black pens and the unused blue ones
the closet door that's never quite shut
What do you think of?

One day I will cease to make sense.
My words that once held
so much wisdom
so much emotion
so much meaning
will become nothing more than a thing of the past.
My lust for legacy,
when will it end?

www.ingramcontent.com/pod-product-compliance
Lightning Source LLC
Chambersburg PA
CBHW072013290426
44109CB00018B/2221